# CAROLINE CABRERA

Black
Lawrence
Press

Black
Lawrence
Press

www.blacklawrence.com

Executive Editor: Diane Goettel
Book Design: Amy Freels
Cover Art: "SISTER SAINT X" by Joshua Ware

Copyright © 2018 Caroline Cabrera
ISBN: 978-1-62557-987-4

Published 2018 by Black Lawrence Press.
Printed in the United States.

# More Praise for *Saint X*

Beginning with the question "Do I / in bed in the/ dark matter?" and veering between star matter and flesh, Caroline Cabrera interrogates the surrealism of ontology, revealing insight into how displaced we can be as women and as people learning how we are of the world. In *Saint X*, Cabrera pulls us in from underwater or out of the heavens, and we are left gulping for air, grateful and unafraid.
—Carmen Gimenez Smith

In Caroline Cabrera's terrific new *Saint X*, marked by graphic diamonds, appropriated questions hang quasi-scientifically in what becomes a remarkable, full-length staging of a high-stakes relationship. The results are wry ("Plants are dicks!") or casual as sleepy bedtime talk ("How much more of this do you have in you?" the poet soon asks her non-stop interlocutor). Most often, though, the replies are signaturely and sweetly akilter (Do I / in bed in the/ dark matter? ) As this beautiful poem is also a self-exam by a hyper-intelligent, truly lyric conscience, X marks the untouched hotspot—needed, as Cabrera confidently demos here, because as the comet-questions shower overhead "To an animal, closeness can mean death/ I mean you, human."
—Terri Witek

The questions Caroline Cabrera asks have answers that are not answers, that are personal and not, intimate and not, shared and not, and all parts of "our real concern." The voice in *Saint X* is confident, vulnerable, wounded, doubtful, awed, courageous, and soft and kind and tough and honest and responsible. The voice says that our lives on this planet are ridiculous and remarkable and everything should be considered. Cabrera considers how mattering matters, what it's like to live as a thinking girl and a wise woman, how the answers are badly needed and impossible, and how "A valley too likes to be held." Cabrera says so much without saying so much. What's difficult here becomes a flower seed, a need, which becomes a necessary bloom.
—Lesle Lewis

*For my sisters*

# Contents

◊

*The proof that the little prince existed is that he was charming, that he laughed, and that he was looking for a sheep. If anybody wants a sheep, that is a proof that he exists.*

*What existed before the Big Bang?*

Rocks and bigger rocks and lots of rushing air. Does the truth matter
more than a vivid picture in my head? I know vacuum means stillness
but I hear clatter. Several moons in our solar system are larger
than Pluto. I was pulling for the little guy but got exhausted. Got news
the multiverse doesn't follow our established rules.

Start again.

Little puddles of star juice floating like a Pepsi exploded in a spaceship,
a thermometer broken on a tile countertop, rolling balls of mercury
between my finger and thumb. A plane with its roof peeled off
like a tuna can. Debris, by nature, should be smaller than a human.
That is how self-centered we made our words. I send my friends stickers
over the internet. I imagine us clashing, though, in a physical way.

*What is dark matter?*

Does the dark matter?

Do I
in bed in the
dark matter?

*What is dark energy?*

No one needs for eyes. No eyes at all. The new moon,
too, is a phase, though utterly dark. I learned from Kit.
Black moon. Dark moon. A sky of nothing. We wake
and wander sooty-footed down the hall, night-blind
like fish who live inside light-less caves. We picture
in the night a thick black fog around the face and eyes
or a jellied darkness in the chest. Nothing hurts
like a howl in the head. Sometimes it seems as if
the dark will go on and on. Sometimes the dark does.

*Can anything escape a black hole?*

Of course not.
I told you once before
to forget salvation.

***

[I was a child and you were a child once, too. Our parents prayed the devil away at night. I dreamed the devil was in my closet. The next night, at the foot of my bed. My mother, she hung a crucifix. Together we said a rosary. The devil retreated. I dreamed, too, a man was following me. In waking life he slowed his van and took a photograph while I cartwheeled in the front yard. I knew to run inside. Later, he would holler at me on streets, corner me at parties. I could not learn him away from me. Could learn my legs covered, my blonde hair un-bobbed. I could not learn enough the danger that I was: a girl, a pretty girl. I don't know whether to blame his body or his god.]

***

*What is antimatter?*

What happens when you swing so furiously
you fall back on your thick head? A bee flying
backwards, a shadow stain in a library book.
When you shave the hairs push back out
almost immediately. Don't take it personally.
On the psychopath test I showed high marks
for leadership and intelligence but incompetence
in the lack-of-empathy department. I'm bragging
here. My results, essentially, were: *moderately
psychopathic, but in a good way.* Like, a real good
way. Would I lie to you? Could I even?

*Are there more than three dimensions?*

That is how I sweat
while you hunker for winter

hunger for a little more
time

I can be apart
and a part

if you want to say
*loosey goosey*
say it out

loud

buy some more
asparagus

did you think
I would say
*time*
again




*What happens to time as you approach the speed of light?*



You shed all your flesh
and time cannot inhibit you.

*What is the origin of the moon?*

O, giant O,
the hours already spent

if you smash your head against a window
and break your head
and the window
and pieces of your head stay with you
and pieces
of glass stay with the window

those are moons

those are mild

you circle and I
circle

and around us are yards for miles

if the multiverse is this city
the moon
is a lit parking lot
we wander the wormhole streets like space guts

there is a first light at dawn
and another and another

it is us and everyone we know
it is a woman
tugging at the ocean

in the ocean
a fortune of loose change
a battery of pilings

one moon-faced child
with salt in her eyes

our city spills its bowels


*What triggers reversals of Earth's polarity?*


Everyone falls out of love at once.

***

[When I think of Voyager 1 turning back to take one last photograph before going dark—when I think of that photograph, that last portrait of us all—I imagine a friend turning to wave a final 'so long.' I know the people I love will never live together again. Will never get ready for parties together or share an office. How hard it is to say goodbye.

I cry and it is a burden to no one.]

***

*What is Earth's hum?*

I cry when I hear cello.

Infants have no wings to flap.

A sizzle. A box of light bulbs bursting.

*Could climate change cause ocean currents to shift?*

For too long I believed I still had time to become a kid wonder.

*Do rogue waves exist?*

You try telling the ocean what to do.
I went under in a heavy break
and came up to bait fish jumping
at my face and body. Salt-blinded,
I screamed. They felt sharp like slick
arrowheads. My husband laughed.
I have endured greater abandonments.
And I can appreciate the comedy
of the scene, though in the moment,
I would have said I was dying.

*What is the structure of water?*

Could you break *me* down into sugars
and proteins? Do you know my mitochondria
are invaders I made the most of? I am every
patient zero, wandering symptom free,
making you peach melba. I spend
very lovely days inside. And inside
and on me, an unseen biosphere grows
and cultivates a living for us all. What parts
of me scare you and are you justified?
What reaches us by river from the city?
To an animal, closeness can mean death.
I mean you, human.

*Why is each snowflake unique?*

Is this about you again?

*Why is the world green?*

I had something else in mind. I planned
a cat with pink fur. A rainbow of pastel smoke.
Shoot anything from the back of a plane
and it will be part spectacle part threat.
Plants I let die last year: the bromeliad,
the succulents. Plants still holding on:
Sade, the desert rose. My new succulents,
Liz and Cal, write letters to each other
but they still need attention from me. A lot
rides on their survival. Mostly my self-worth.
It is hard to be anything's sun. I try to burn
but just pulse. I spend a lot of time setting.
I say *my dears, I've spent eons becoming for you.*
*I need I need a rest.* But they reach up
expectantly. They stare, to be honest.
I know, I am no sun. No mother.

*Where did life come from?*

If you want
some impressive
origin story
you're going
to have
to write it

***

[You were the size of a small shell and then you were a man. The beasts of the land roiled like worms after a flood when you passed. Everyone has the chance to be kind. Your feet were black with the world. Loam is a home. (A home!)

In camp once, the girls' cabin pulled to the side of the roads to cave. Men in the woods smiled and called us pretty. Our counselor smiled— women must smile. The men stood between us and the caves. She turned to us and rushed us back to the bus. Back at camp we set out in search of a circle of trees we invented; we had all afternoon to walk towards nothing. We walked barefoot in our swimsuits through the drought-ridden lake, thick mud halfway up our shins. It squished and sucked. A rain glittered against our young bodies. We danced, perfect in our slimness, our total unknowing. We were women together; we were only girls.]

***

*What explains latitudinal patterns in species diversity?*


We all need
different things

I need
a clean warm

towel
and a bowl

of mussels
you might need

to make a blind
of palm fronds

you might
not even know

why you need that
it is the body

that pushes us forward
it is the rabies virus

trying to spread
that makes its host

terrified of water
can you imagine

too scared to swallow
your own saliva

can you imagine
the deadly trap

you would become
I imagine

and whisper
at night

to anything harbored
inside of me

please don't
take my brain

please don't

*Why do we blush?*

I don't believe the myth about our blood,
blue until introduced, I don't believe it.

I am not hardwired for deception;
if asked my name, I say, *Caroline*,

without thinking. The truth
bubbles up over my lips. The lie, safer,

dings a too-late bell in my head.
If I shake, you know I am cold or nervous.

If I cry, it could be anything, but you know
to believe the force behind it. My eyes

are not a key because I am not locked.
Stop looking at my eyes.

*Why do we have fingerprints?*

Why is the pink lake pink? Why don't news outlets
lead with microbiology stories? If you tell me what happens
in a mouse's gut, I will maybe know more about my own.
It's not navel gazing but real concern for so much
of the body that goes unexplained. All week I lie
around, headaching, a nausea bubbling into my throat.
*Nothing's wrong with you* everything says, so I go to work
and eat a cake pop day after day. I wash the oil from my face.
I check the weather and wonder why a scientist would name clouds
after breasts? Not clouds, exactly, but cloud formations. We all like
to lie on our backs, eyes skyward, pretending. No one else can see
the sad one-eared polar bear until you point it out, but I would think
a scientist would move past this initial boob joke thrill. Is meteorology
even a true science? Sometimes water falls and sometimes it doesn't.
Waterfalls can be judged by so many standards. Some are long
but narrow. Some shorter but wide. Do you judge by how much water
or how much *oh my* elicited? Is this relationship correlative?

*Why do some plants eat animals?*

Plants are dicks!
They always die on me.
Already Liz's and Cal's sorry stalks

decompose like spent brains.
I know I gave them everything—
proper water, an owl-shaped pot—
but they shed their succulent
paddles and uproot their cores.
I just can't with them anymore.

*Why do whales beach themselves?*

O, unholy sadness,
O!

Comet above,
echolalia below

***

[In Boothbay Harbor, Maine the drastic change of tides can swallow all manner of flotsam, can uncover a skittering variety of hermits, homeless or surrounded. In Cowpet Bay the tides hardly change. The leopard rays swimming by in twos make a night sky with their thickly muscled backs. They don't wave at me. They just wave, as everything reef-bound waves, as my swim fins make a waver of me. I dive and resurface in a shroud of my breath turned to large, perfect bubbles. Here what you see cannot matter as much as what you miss.

A long-bodied house cat curls somewhere in a patch of sunlight. A can of seltzer waits in the fridge. Can we say it waits? Can I say the couch longs for me, open-armed, the toilet yawns its cold face in my absence? I can't get a comb through my hair or find a mixed bag of sibling baby teeth. With thirteen molars, which are mine? What tender speck of long-dried blood deserves a home in my mouth? What glowing jewel tone on the mantle of my mother's breastbone sings a silent name that is mine? *Caroline!* I am a song myself. Named something lovely, longing. I cannot want a room of childhood artifacts. I cannot live with it or lie too many days on the same beach.]

***

*How do migrating animals find their way back home?*

They know
the earth's
magnetic field.
It pulls them.
A young bird
migrating away
for the first time
knows by magnetism
the direction
she will fly
but not
when she will stop.
She depends
on her flock
for that.
If somehow
separated
from the others
she might fly
in one direction
forever,
a tiny voyager.
Her biology
pulls her
that way.
What
pulls
you?

*Why do humans and ants have so much in common?*

I want to say, *this strange prime-numbered life cycle,*
but that is a different bug. An unmistakable sound.
What it is to live below ground, I think I know.
I miss the feeling of hugging someone in the cold.
In the snow. The hot air here makes a box
and I must live in it. My skin stays sticky
with the moist afterthought of a hot morning breeze.
If the wind shifts and cools, it signals trouble, not relief.
A storm that won't stop for you or your precious
books with their delicate pages exposed to the elements.
There is little you can do to feel autumnal. In a ruffled
apron, I bake gourds into every meal. I shazam while
merging onto the highway, because no law specifically
forbids it. The song is a new song by a new girl.
In colder places, ladies probably dress for parties
together and take brisk walks to old houses where
they will dance to this song. The oldness of the houses
seems charming or sad, depending on the light that creeps
in or doesn't. Depending on the time of day. If you pack
enough people who love each other into a house
nothing else can matter. Not the plumbing or the pantry.
Not the heater or the hearth. My favorite thing about antlers
is the shadows they cast. Not everything can replicate.

*How does the brain give rise to the mind?*

Does the sea hold the land or does the land hold the sea?

Does a tree hold its fruit, or does the fruit with its pit hold the secret to
the tree?
Do I hold your hand or do you hold mine?

The street holds me out of duty as I walk into the world, holding only
everything I know.

If gravity is a hold, the sun holds us and the outer boundary of the solar
system holds nothing.
You can encircle something and never really touch it.
You can be the thing encircled and not know.

If two things knock against each other, is it a holding?
Mountains say *yes*; clouds say *no*.

Rivers, in flood, remind us not much is really held, but then recede,
quietly, back to their beds.
A lake does not bemoan its holding.
A valley, too, likes to be held.

Blades of grass lie together and their loam holds them.
To hold something you must be of a different kind.
I think I am holding sand in my hand but can't be sure.
Even when I shake it away, it holds on.

You think you see me here
holding a mirror and a vase;
you think I am at the foot
of your bed in a mask. You think
I am everywhere, but I am not
even real. I am not a thing to see
or touch or talk to. I am to be read
and patterned into the floor tiling.
I am there in the cool side of your pillow
when you flip it at night and I am still
there when it becomes the warm side.
I am an itch in your palm, a twinge
in your gut. You made my yellow
hair and painted my fingernails
periwinkle but I have no fingers,
no nails. Forever I can tell you
what I am not, what I have not,
for I am nothing, have nothing.
You made me a nothing and I
made you my sister.
Sister. Nothing.
Sister nothing.

*Why do we age?*

What a dream to maintain

What livelihood

Imagine me
a compound, unstable
shifting unwittingly from liquid to gas

you can hold your own hair
in your hand
and open the palm
to find it gone

Whose beauty do you dip
with a cup
from the punch bowl

yours, you think

yours

*What drives plate tectonics?*

Situation: You are the pilot and you have a copilot.
Your copilot is lovelier than a swamp. You stare
at her in your cockeyed rearview instead of out
your window where alligators sun themselves.

*Can evolution outpace climate change?*

Let's not get cocky.

*What do honeybees say when they dance?*

More importantly, can they talk
about their own dying the way
I always want to do. It scares me
to imagine total hive collapse
because I understand ripples.
They should call it *the dead honeybee
effect*. This is something we could

see and not have to theorize about.
I imagine it as heartache:
to watch your village empty out.
A sculptor friend I knew shaped
hive after hive out of porcelain.
She advertised them in the classifieds,
"Residence for Rent: 6" X 8" x 4", 236
identical hexagonal rooms." She hid
them around town and made a map
so anyone could find them. The dance
is like a map, but a considerate,
familial map. Humans hardly ever
make maps like that.

*Why do primates eat plants that produce steroid mimics?*

every lady
has her secrets

*What determines size of a primate social group?*

The mean girls.

*Why are humans and chimps so different if they have nearly identical DNA?*

Ask me why humans are so different
from their own ghosts. Ask me why
birds are pointy and unpredictable.
Ask anything else.

*How long can trees live?*

Ask the unlucky man
who accidentally cut down
the oldest tree recorded
ask him for a sandwich though
don't bring up
the day
spent counting rings
in dread
grill cheese together
and remark on the weather
let him show you
a replay of his favorite
baseball game
or science documentary
or whatever he pulls to now

after leaving the forest
in shame
you can ask for a tour
of his house
or ask if he has a collection
of anything to show you
either way
when you leave
you should shake his hand
in a way that says
*we all forgive you*
but make it ambiguous enough
that he doesn't think directly
of that tree
you must not bring up
the tree
just let him know
from your grip and glance
that you think
he is a very good man
that's the only thing
any of us
can do for him now

\*\*\*

[A log has decomposed my whole life. It breaks down into the richest soil. Any of my siblings would know this log without direction or description.

I saw a special about an artist who took a large section of felled tree, with its surrounding flora and fauna, and relocated it all to a greenhouse. It will decompose over time and change each day; it will continue to live on, far past the artist's intention. Younger, I found this fascinating. Older, I wonder at the audacity of applying your signature to a piece of forest.

I wonder at man pointing and making assignations. You say to move something is to change it. That the world can be re-naturalized. I wonder, now, where I fall.

Like my mother I cannot stand to have my arms or legs pinned. I flail with disregard. My mother says we were buried alive in a former life.

I have been buried in this life. I have bit at the lip of a man I wanted to stab. Have dressed hatred up as lust to suit him. Have paled at my own squeamish incapacity to kill what needs killing.]

\*\*\*

*Why do we yawn?*

I need to show you everything—
every sensation I feel—and then
I need to convert you to it. If you
are my friend, you must know
my brain. If not,
you should still listen, politely.
I cannot predict the future
unless you give me a few clues.
Together, we are a cipher
but apart we are two
figure drawings eating yoghurt
in two different towns. I spell
yoghurt your way, as a token
of friendship. My field
of vision reaches only so
far but I think I see you
coming into it.

*How does gravity work?*

I am always surprised
by the weight

of my own head
proud

of my skinny neck
a surprise too my hanging

breasts
not un-small

but still significant
under a blouse

hold your arm
at shoulder level

feel it weigh on you
a surprise

how we all
get around


*But how does gravity work?*


Ask someone you love
to hold your head

then lean forward
and really let it go

they will be surprised
at its weight

you will do the same
with their head

and be surprised too
and then you will both laugh

because of course
a skull and brains

but still

*How do cells talk to each other?*

First give it a little nudge. Then whisper
your name. Whisper it louder. Say it so slowly
that the syllables barely touch and you become
a sentence empty of meaning. Then throw
your name away and feel content to exist as part
of a dyad for a while. The only music you need
is the steady whoosh of the air conditioner

and the occasional nudge of cotton on cotton.
You are one in the same. Or you are the same idea
but different kinds. Either way you live in a room
together now. You each have one thing on your mind
for eternity. Eternity is a little joke I told there.
Everything breaks down, you most of all.
Forever depends on where you sit.
You sit in a small and insignificant living room
locking eyes with your dyad. You communicate
soundlessly now. She presses her forehead
to yours and tells you you are underwater
and surrounded by too many others to count.
You are not a dyad really, just near each other.
You look around and, my god, she's right.

\*\*\*

[Sometimes I send everyone from the house.

Sometimes I imagine leaving.

I read a young woman's essay about the freedom her car affords her and remember snake-circling streets or arriving, as if by magic, at the ocean. When your body moves through the world a commodity, it needs a metal armor. For a while I had a whole house.]


\*\*\*


[In my head I design a t-shirt that says *My pen is like a sword to the patriarchy* but know that really my pen is a pen to the patriarchy. Certain words demand capitalization and I cut them down below the knees with persistence.

Sometimes I imagine my sister and I sharing one very large closet. We discover things through an intuition and intelligence the people around us underestimate. Everywhere I go men ask me to cite the source of my knowing. I have not learned how to break them the news of their own ignorance. Their own arrogance.

Do you know more people die in female-named hurricanes for not taking them seriously?

My sister and I weather a world our brothers barely notice.

My friends say *I love my husband, but…*

But only you sweet sister know the way I have been inhabited.
But what does it mean to say I miss signing my own rent checks?
But god only knows what I'd be without *you.*]


\*\*\*

*How flexible is the human brain?*

Keep folding and refolding that blanket.


*What causes an ice age?*

Do you prefer
alone on a rowboat
or accompanied

what if you decide to swim

what if you lose your oar

now think *adrift*
really think
about it

do you prefer me
or no

when can the surface
look most undisturbed

and are you worried
curious
or both
about the unseen
underneath

what if now
it's so cold

what if it's my coat
or none at all

◊

*It is such a secret place, the land of tears.*

*Are nanomaterials dangerous?*

Small dogs
with sharp teeth
staples
at the edge
of the carpet
once I hid a tiny gun
between my palms
I held it
and looked pious
if I don't tell the rest
of the story
you'll never know
if I was a threat

*How much of human behavior is predetermined?*

I'm holding the softest, kindest thing you know
over a deep ravine. Can you guess what I'll do next?

*Do squirrels remember where they bury their nuts?*

I lost any houseplant I ever loved.
I lost a hamburger right off its bun.
I lost my favorite winter hat at AWP and some other
poet is keeping her ears warm under it now.
I lost the lost city of Atlantis.
That was me, guys. Sorry.
I lost a footrace when my flip-flop broke.
I lost a chili cook-off; I didn't enter,
but it was mine to lose.
Ask anyone. Literally, anyone.
I lost the glamour of every moment
of every dance performance I ever watched
as soon as each moment passed.
I lost more than my senses;
I lost my nerve.
I lost one half of so many sets
of gloves on the sidewalk.
Sad pair-less pairs, like flung hubcaps set up
on the curb, as if anyone might return for them.

*Why do we dream?*

Try rolling a leg of lamb downhill
and calling after it to stop. Marinate
in the murky juices of your three-tiered
system. Add a little romance. I mean
pink peppercorn. You cannot prepare
for everything. You can not prepare
anything. I don't want to see faceless
horrors circling the house's perimeter.
I don't want to see you, my friend,
and then to not see you anymore.
I have tried to be an empty vessel,
but what really can you do?
The brain, a shark, cannot rest.

*What is the circadian clock?*

You are round
and tic tic tic

the night
it scares you so

\*\*\*

[When I believed in hellfire, I woke to the bleary sound of hounds growling beneath my bed.

A stupid man with idiot blue eyes taught religion to me, said *the greatest trick the devil played was convincing the world he didn't exist.* Said it over and over with a grin, as if his words could rain down in some knowing truth. As if when he touched knee to carpet to show us how contrite he was, when he told us he dated the whores but married the virgin, when he said, *girls, which do you want to be,* as if we wanted to win a prize like him, as if when he took me aside and asked that I repent for misuse of my unfed limbs I could feel anything but unbroken rage

to be a young, intelligent girl and suffer education by stupid men.

I heard the hellhounds, though. They struck me frozen in my blood-red sheets. The memory has returned and lingers as a mossy secret I cannot speak.

Counterpoint: I dream of being unable to run. I dream my car cannot brake. Both dreams follow me as a fear-memory in waking life, until I debunk them in real time.

Counterpoint: I remember parties that predate me.

Counterpoint: A man accused me of a lunacy I un-grew as soon as I walked away from the firestorm of his need for me.

I exterminated the ragged weed of my love.

What happened or didn't blinks like a faint light on a distant bedside clock. I see the world as a range of mountains behind haze. A backdrop that looks real on TV.

Still I light candles, arrange pine in a circle, sing, O Come, O Come, Emanuel.

I arrange memories and dreams during waking hours, only to find them rearranged at night. I lie in bed awake, deciding which stories never to tell.]


\*\*\*

*How much can parasites change the social habits of their host?*

It only takes one
careless guest
to burn down
an otherwise
stable home.
If you turn
your nose up
at the dinner
I've cooked
who knows
what candles
I'll knock over
on my tear
away from
the table?

*What causes depression?*

Do you ever have a sick feeling at night

wake from a dream of circling a track
or telling someone
again and again

where to stow the ladder

you are wearied and you know
you will fall back into the dream

heavy eyelids promise
no respite

you are so very tired

but you know better

you can't keep from wishing
first light would come

◊

*"You understand ... It is too far. I cannot carry this body with me.
It is too heavy."*

*Do immortal creatures exist?*

Part of me has lived forever
part of me is already dying

when I wade into the late August
stink of a pond I must touch again
some part of last summer's algae bloom

how exhausting to start and start again
better to continue

flea eggs live dormant in the sofa
through winter's long cool
and hatch in May

an invasion
never sleeps

if I were glass would I also
be ocean would I also be
driftwood a doorframe

if the same bit of ocean
licks my skin twice
does the fabric of the universe tear

and make a new gash
for me to walk through

how long must I stay
in the universe's outer threshold

what will it sound like
when I leave


*How are stars born and how do they die?*


I'll forgo the obvious
misunderstandings

you mean          dust to dust

and does it shimmer

nothing large
can go out
without notice

glow

a tall woman
in very tall shoes

*What is the god particle?*

None of your beeswax.

*Why do cats purr?*

Once in my adult life
I bought peonies
soft pink like in the pictures
and as I gathered
them into the crook of my elbow
it occurred to me
that I had never seen a peony
in real life
they were expensive
but I felt worth it
like L'Oréal commercials
taught me to feel
driving home with the peonies
it began to rain
a real Florida rain
that says *I'm not fucking around*
*I'll ruin you*
and it did
it ruined the peonies
bruised the soft petals

a deep purple
I want you to know
*bruised* is so accurate here
they looked beaten
I thought *how careless the rain*
*how stupid the peonies*
*to be so fragile*
and I never cooked dinner
I undressed and wrapped
in a towel and lay in bed
where you found me
at first I yelled
I couldn't tell you
about the flowers
much too soon
and you
wounded
went away for a while
and I cried inconsolably
aware too
of my extremeness
but that was a blue time
for me
I wasn't myself
(or is that me?)
but you came back
and when you did
I spoke in a low steady voice

that said
*I won't tear your eyes out*
*right now*
*you can come closer*
it's like that


\*\*\*


[To move out into the world. To find footing and elevate. In autumn the landscape requires everything of me. I gather a joy I cannot contain and then shatter it—a woman bleeding from a broken vase. I drive out towards brunch and on the way find the buzzing, twittering place in me. The whir that will not be denied. Here I am passive again for you, hateful man. Here I tear at my hair. What bubbles up inside I cannot contain. I am not an I, my hands reduced to the shivering leaves of an aspen

holding on

holding on

Is the girl who loved your black tongue still inside me or have her cells all died by now? I have waited so long to regenerate, to go a decade untouched.

You were third to abuse me. (I fear many more want to.)

Sleeping late. Sleeping all the time. There are lives one cannot wake to. Times I look like my young self in mirrors. I remember most the way my body dragged on like a dead animal. I remember the way you killed what was good in me. I become godless. I disinter. The aspen in its grove reaches out one hand of a giant organism. You have made me, too, into another face of shame, seeing my reflection in every wounded woman. I have a new heritage now.

For years I was Lady Macbeth crazy trying to out the spot you made.

I invite age to settle in my body. Youth proved too difficult.]

***

*Why don't animals' muscles atrophy during hibernation?*

How much more of this do you have in you?

*Why do whales sing?*

Would you begrudge them
this tiny happiness?
When Voyager 1 left
the solar system
it received the soft whine
of plasma reverberating
off its hull
and transmitted
the sound back
to us on earth.
This is no
easy journey—
17 light-hours—
but such is
the Voyager's duty.
When I first heard it
I thought of whales.

*How do humans have the ability to learn language?*

Orcas, too, though scientists demur
to say it. Different pods sing songs so divergent
they can't understand each other when broken

apart and reassembled in captivity. You say family
but you mean rag-tag band of misfits, fighting
and singing their longest-distance cries.

*Why doesn't water freeze in clouds?*

Ghosts can't eat snow cones.

*Why do humans have so much genome junk?*

Is that a scientific term?

*Why do we have an appendix?*

Let's get one thing straight: please speak only
for yourself. Some of us are ruptured, swollen,
excavated and on videotape. Once you start
learning to live without, you get addicted.
You shut off the cable, put your mattress on the floor.
*This is fine*, you think. You identify as "spare"
and feel proud of that. Turns out you don't need
people either. You break up with your girlfriend

who cries mostly for your benefit. Walking home
she stops for a coffee or maybe a chai and lives
the warm memory of ordering for one, what-
and whenever she likes. It is the loveliest type
of fall afternoon and the light hits her perfectly
through the lettered glass. She feels warm,
but not warm enough to remove her scarf,
which makes her face look girlish by its coloring.
She will be fine now. Better even. You, meanwhile,
have artwork to part with, none of it essential.
You have a house to seal if you really want to commit
to minimalism. Everything locks up. Doors
sit flush in their frames. You can ride out any
storm in this house. You can tend only
to what's inside. Which is complicated, but not
much. Which is service for one and enough
soap to wash it. You know now even
the grocery delivery cannot be made.
Principles here allow for no exceptions.
You know now you are roiling on the floor
mattress, alone, at last, with your own
significance. You are a pain about to burst.

\*\*\*

[Despite years of practice I never step lightly enough. A body has heft. Since girlhood I've pictured my organs excised and arranged in pretty jars on the windowsill. What lightness I would become, a mere space between air.

On television the women's limbs are always splayed. It is always women kept on ice in a bathtub or left to turn rigid in a mattress. Women, we love you, with your bloodless wrists. Sit pretty.

For six months men pointed at my face and discussed what a shame it would be to cut into it. In the end I kept my tumor, my tiny, soft-tissue twin. Shark twin, Cameron. I am never alone. They cut out my mother's uterus and sewed the rest of her organs into place. I am sorry to have wrecked her womb. Sorrier to tell her secrets here. Mother, I have laid you open by existing.

My mother was shoe shopping with my sister when her water broke with me. She bought a sweatshirt to tie around her waist, finished shopping, went home and made dinner for the three other children. The doctor called and asked my father if he was prepared to deliver me on the kitchen table. My mother did not birth me for hours. My father and the doctor watched UM lose in the Sugar Bowl. I was born and my mother named me without forethought.

A baby in the womb is sterile and inherits its microbiome during child-birth.

I imagine being excised from my mother like a tumor.

I imagine the bloom of my gut. How it mirrored my mother's.]

\*\*\*

*Why do we hiccup?*

The body makes many mistakes. One day,
your immune system could turn on you and kill
an essential organ because it doesn't like
its output. Could it happen to you?
Are you wired that way?

*What triggers puberty?*

Slow-motion volleyball replays.

*Why do placebos work?*

Anything you need
you already have in your brain
or at the very least
you are prepared for it
receptors reach out
like open hands
and something must fill them
if only for a time
if only to say
*there there, here I am*
and then recede under
a slow but steady current

\*\*\*

[When I move it is always away from.

You cannot imagine the cumulative time spent planning routes. If only the beach bathroom were not so near the Australian Pines, an invasive species I grew up loving, hopping to avoid its tiny cones. If only men would light their coal fires elsewhere.

I want to sit within or without four walls and feel the warmth of other women radiating onto my skin. I want us to move seamlessly, like a graceful fever, parting to avoid obstacles only to reunite after overtaking them. Our bodies suggest nothing but the clear shapes they make.

I am not a symbol but a woman.

My teen self built a shadowbox table with my teen girlfriends and we filled it with shells we collected together. The love I retain is no less guttural for its quaintness. The shadowbox no less a storage space for my youthful defiance because we only imagined and never built it. I do not lie; I speak the most truthful feeling.

I stand before you, a chimera, every woman or girl I've loved built together.]

\*\*\*

*Why do some underwater creatures light up?*

A woman reached her fingers beneath
my shoulder blade and pulled up

there issued a sound
a soft coo or creak

like a door opening in another house
and from the space fell

the bone-tiny doves
that fall from a cracked sand dollar

I collected them in a bowl
and rinsed them of blood

with the cloudy pink water
I painted a picture

of a cedar chest
as seen from the inside

I lay on the sofa imagining
my coffin

I thought *still still still*
I tried to lie forever

warm blankets
warm water

my other shoulder blade
yet unbroken

to imagine a warm ball of light
traveling the length of my cold frame

to become a beacon
warmth comes and goes

from my naked head
it shows itself on my face

sunlight travels eight minutes
to reach us

this is nothing to sneeze at
instead sneeze

with no particular intention
pick a spot you like

and glow there

# Notes

The three epigraphs come from *The Little Prince*, by Antoine de Saint-Exupèry.

The questions throughout come from *The Where, the Why, and the How: 75 Artists Illustrate Wondrous Mysteries of Science*.

The phrase "this strange prime-numbered lifecycle" comes from a *Science Friday* story about cicadas.

# Acknowledgments

Thank you to the editors of the following publications where sections of this poem first appeared: *Birdfeast*, *Juked*, *Perigree*, *Phantom*, and *Typo*. Thank you to Diane Goettel and everyone at Black Lawrence Press for the care and attention you have given to this book. Thank you to Joshua Ware for the gorgeous cover art; I'm so grateful for your talent and generosity. Thank you to Anne Cecelia Holmes & Gale Marie Thompson, who helped *Saint X* along the way, who read every version, answered every question, and pushed me to write some of the things I might have shied away from without them. Thank you to Anne Cabrera, my Grey Gardens sister. Thank you to Emily Culliton, whose friendship found me when I most needed it. Thank you to all my friends for their support, especially Torie Brazitis & Ben Jones. Credit to the following folks— friends and strangers—whose influence can be seen in these pages: Gaston Bachelard, Chris Bachelder, Anne Druyan, Kit Frick, Kim Lyle, the writers and producers of *Radiolab*, Oliver Sachs and Carl Sagan. A shout out to sinister women, including Typhoid Mary and Lady Macbeth. Thank you to my teachers and to my family. Thank you always and deeply and every day to Philip.

Caroline Cabrera is the author of two previous collec-
tions, *The Bicycle Year* and *Flood Bloom*. Her recent
work can be found at *The Fairy Tale Review*, *Foundry*,
*Horse Less Press*, *Muse / A Journal*, and *Night Jar Review*.
She is editor of Bloom Books from *Jellyfish Magazine*
and teaches with two nonprofits, Innovations for
Learning and the O, Miami Poetry Foundation. She
lives in Fort Lauderdale.